REVIEW COPY
COURTESY OF
ENSLOW PUBLISHERS, INC.

STATES

ALABAMA
A MyReportLinks.com Book

Marylou Morano Kjelle

MyReportLinks.com Books
an imprint of
 Enslow Publishers, Inc.
Box 398, 40 Industrial Road
Berkeley Heights, NJ 07922
USA

MyReportLinks.com Books, an imprint of Enslow Publishers, Inc. MyReportLinks is a trademark of Enslow Publishers, Inc.

Copyright © 2003 by Enslow Publishers, Inc.

All rights reserved.

No part of this book may be reproduced by any means without the written permission of the publisher.

Library of Congress Cataloging-in-Publication Data

Kjelle, Marylou Morano.
  Alabama / Marylou Morano Kjelle.
    p. cm. — (States)
  Summary: Discusses the land and climate, economy, government, and history of the state of Alabama. Includes Internet links to Web sites.
  Includes bibliographical references and index.
  ISBN 0-7660-5151-X
  1. Alabama—Juvenile literature. [1. Alabama.] I. Title. II. States (Series : Berkeley Heights, N.J.)
  F326.3.K58 2003
  976.1—dc21
                              2002153557

Printed in the United States of America

10 9 8 7 6 5 4 3 2 1

To Our Readers:
Through the purchase of this book, you and your library gain access to the Report Links that specifically back up this book.
The Publisher will provide access to the Report Links that back up this book and will keep these Report Links up to date on **www.myreportlinks.com** for three years from the book's first publication date.
We have done our best to make sure all Internet addresses in this book were active and appropriate when we went to press. However, the author and the Publisher have no control over, and assume no liability for, the material available on those Internet sites or on other Web sites they may link to.
The usage of the MyReportLinks.com Books Web site is subject to the terms and conditions stated on the Usage Policy Statement on **www.myreportlinks.com**.
A password may be required to access the Report Links that back up this book. The password is found on the bottom of page 4 of this book.
Any comments or suggestions can be sent by e-mail to comments@myreportlinks.com or to the address on the back cover.

Photo Credits: © 2001 Robesus, Inc., p. 10; © Corel Corporation, p. 3; Alabama Bureau of Tourism and Travel, pp. 13, 23; Alabama Bureau of Tourism and Travel/Dan Brothers, pp. 11, 22, 24, 27, 32; Alabama Bureau of Tourism and Travel/Karim Shamsi-Basha, p. 20; Alabama Department of Archives and History, pp. 35, 39, 41; Birmingham Civil Rights Institute, p. 15; Enslow Publishers, pp. 1, 19; Ivy Green, the Birthplace of Helen Keller, p. 16; Library of Congress, pp. 31, 45; MyReportLinks.com Books, p. 4; National Park Service, p. 43; The Marshall Space Flight Center, p. 29.

Cover Photo: © PhotoDisc 1995, Inc.

Cover Description: The State Capitol, Montgomery.

Contents

Report Links 4

Alabama Facts 10

1 The State of Alabama 11

2 Land and Climate 18

3 Economy 26

4 Government 34

5 History 38

Chapter Notes 46

Further Reading 47

Index 48

About MyReportLinks.com Books

MyReportLinks.com Books
Great Books, Great Links, Great for Research!

MyReportLinks.com Books present the information you need to learn about your report subject. In addition, they show you where to go on the Internet for more information. The pre-evaluated Report Links that back up this book are kept up to date on **www.myreportlinks.com**. With the purchase of a MyReportLinks.com Books title, you and your library gain access to the Report Links that specifically back up that book. The Report Links save hours of research time and link to dozens—even hundreds—of Web sites, source documents, and photos related to your report topic.

Please see "To Our Readers" on the Copyright page for important information about this book, the MyReportLinks.com Books Web site, and the Report Links that back up this book.

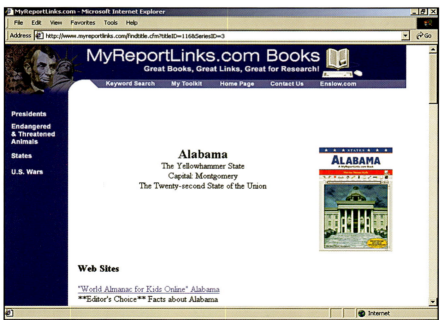

Access:

The Publisher will provide access to the Report Links that back up this book and will try to keep these Report Links up to date on our Web site for three years from the book's first publication date. Please enter **SAL8421** if asked for a password.

Tools　Search　Notes　Discuss　▶ MyReportLinks.com Books　Go!

Report Links

> The Internet sites described below can be accessed at
> http://www.myreportlinks.com

*Editor's choice

▶ World Almanac for Kids Online: Alabama

The *World Almanac for Kids Online* Web site provides essential information about Alabama. Here you will learn about the state's land resources, population, government, economy, history, and much more.

Link to this Internet site from http://www.myreportlinks.com

*Editor's choice

▶ Explore the States: Alabama

America's Story from America's Library, a Library of Congress Web site, offers interesting stories about life in Alabama.

Link to this Internet site from http://www.myreportlinks.com

*Editor's choice

▶ U.S. Census Bureau: Alabama

The U.S. Census Bureau Web site contains facts and statistics about Alabama. Here you can explore statistics about population, business, and geography. Click on "Browse more data sets for Alabama" to get more information.

Link to this Internet site from http://www.myreportlinks.com

*Editor's choice

▶ Alabama.gov

Here at the official Web site of the state of Alabama you will find information about Alabama's state government, economy, history, travel, geography, and links to other resources.

Link to this Internet site from http://www.myreportlinks.com

*Editor's choice

▶ Alabama Department of Archives & History

This Web site from the State of Alabama's Department of Archives and History contains an abundance of information on state history, government, geography, population, and symbols.

Link to this Internet site from http://www.myreportlinks.com

*Editor's choice

▶ Alabama State Parks

At the Alabama State Parks Web site you will find descriptions of all of Alabama's state parks. You will also learn about camping, trails, and fishing at these parks.

Link to this Internet site from http://www.myreportlinks.com

Any comments? Contact us: comments@myreportlinks.com

Report Links

 The Internet sites described below can be accessed at
http://www.myreportlinks.com

▶ **African American World: George Washington Carver**
George Washington Carver was an agricultural chemist and agronomist. The work he did while at the Tuskegee Institute in Alabama revolutionized American agriculture. PBS's African American World Reference Room Web site offers a biography of Carver.

Link to this Internet site from http://www.myreportlinks.com

▶ **American Visionaries: Legends of Tuskegee**
This three-part Web exhibit, from the National Park Service, is dedicated to the accomplishments of Booker T. Washington, George Washington Carver, and the Tuskegee Airmen. Founded by Washington, the Tuskegee Institute supported Carver's research and trained the airmen.

Link to this Internet site from http://www.myreportlinks.com

▶ **The Battle of Horseshoe Bend: Collision of Cultures**
This National Park Service Web site explores the Battle of Horseshoe Bend and tells the story of the conflict through articles, maps, and original documents.

Link to this Internet site from http://www.myreportlinks.com

▶ **Birmingham Civil Rights Institute, Alabama USA**
The Birmingham Civil Rights Institute is a museum that traces the civil rights movement from the time of segregation to the present. This site features images and descriptions of the museum's exhibits as well as visitor information.

Link to this Internet site from http://www.myreportlinks.com

▶ **Birthplace of Helen Keller**
As a small child, Helen Keller was afflicted with an illness that left her blind and deaf. Learning to read and write, she dedicated her life to improving the conditions of blind and deaf people. At this Web site you can learn about Keller and her birthplace, Tuscumbia, Alabama.

Link to this Internet site from http://www.myreportlinks.com

▶ **The Boll Weevil Honored in Alabama**
America's Story from America's Library, a Library of Congress Web site, features a story about boll weevils. Entering America in 1892 from Mexico, this destructive insect wreaked havoc in cotton fields throughout the South, including Alabama.

Link to this Internet site from http://www.myreportlinks.com

Any comments? Contact us: **comments@myreportlinks.com**

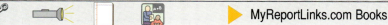

Tools   Search   Notes   Discuss

Report Links

The Internet sites described below can be accessed at
http://www.myreportlinks.com

▶ **Brilliant Careers: Willie Mays**
Westfield, Alabama, native Willie Mays was one of the greatest professional baseball players of all time. This in-depth article profiles Mays's life and career and includes an interview with the star.

Link to this Internet site from http://www.myreportlinks.com

▶ **CWSAC: Battle Summaries**
At this Web site you will find a map showing the sites in Alabama where Civil War battles took place. By clicking on a site, you will find a brief description of that battle.

Link to this Internet site from http://www.myreportlinks.com

▶ **DeSoto's Midwestern Conquest: Starting Point**
In 1540, Spanish explorer Hernando DeSoto reached Alabama. This Web site recounts his travels and discoveries and includes maps and guides to the trails he traveled.

Link to this Internet site from http://www.myreportlinks.com

▶ **George Wallace—Settin' the Woods on Fire**
George Wallace gained international notoriety for his anti-integration policies as governor of Alabama in the 1960s. Over time he changed his views. This American Experience Web site offers a biography of Wallace.

Link to this Internet site from http://www.myreportlinks.com

▶ **Jesse Owens: The Official Web Site**
Olympic gold medalist Jesse Owens of Alabama broke many Olympic and world track and field records. At this official Web site you will find his biography, photographs, and quotations.

Link to this Internet site from http://www.myreportlinks.com

▶ **Mardi Gras in Mobile**
Although Mardi Gras, a celebration that precedes Lent, is typically associated with New Orleans, the first American carnival observance of Mardi Gras was in Mobile. This Library of Congress site contains a short history of Mobile's celebration.

Link to this Internet site from http://www.myreportlinks.com

Any comments? Contact us: comments@myreportlinks.com

Report Links

➤ The Internet sites described below can be accessed at
http://www.myreportlinks.com

▶ **Marshall Space Flight Center**
The Marshall Space Flight Center in Hunstville is where NASA developed the *Saturn V* rocket, which launched the first astronauts to land on the moon. At the center's Web site you will find news, history, science information, and other related resources.

Link to this Internet site from http://www.myreportlinks.com

▶ **The Martin Luther King, Jr., Papers Project**
The Martin Luther King, Jr., Papers Project, from Stanford University's Web site, holds a vast collection of materials related to and written by the civil rights leader.

Link to this Internet site from http://www.myreportlinks.com

▶ **The Official Site of Hank Williams, Sr.**
Born in Georgiana, Alabama, Hank Williams, Sr., is a member of both the Rock and Roll Hall of Fame and the Country Music Hall of Fame. Here you will find his biography, a photo gallery, links, and a list of his hit songs and awards.

Link to this Internet site from http://www.myreportlinks.com

▶ **An Overview of Alabama's Six Constitutions**
The Alabama State Legislature Web site contains a history of Alabama's constitutions. The text of the constitutions and ratification documents, lists of delegates, descriptions of the proceedings, and other resources for each constitution can be found here.

Link to this Internet site from http://www.myreportlinks.com

▶ **Scottsboro: An American Tragedy**
This PBS Web site examines the story of nine African Americans who were falsely accused of raping two white women in Paint Rock, Alabama, in 1931.

Link to this Internet site from http://www.myreportlinks.com

▶ ***Sporting News* Baseball Scrapbook: Hank Aaron**
Mobile's Hank Aaron hit more home runs than any other player in the history of major league baseball. *The Sporting News* Web site contains a time line, photo gallery, articles, career statistics, and much more about the Hall of Fame legend.

Link to this Internet site from http://www.myreportlinks.com

Any comments? Contact us: **comments@myreportlinks.com**

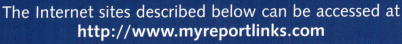

Report Links

The Internet sites described below can be accessed at http://www.myreportlinks.com

▶ **Stately Knowledge: Alabama**
This Web site provides essential facts about Alabama. Here you will learn about historical sites and major industries and can view an image of the state flag.

Link to this Internet site from http://www.myreportlinks.com

▶ **Today In History**
This Library of Congress Web site looks at the life of baseball player Leroy Robert "Satchel" Paige, known as one of the greatest pitchers ever. You will also learn how Leroy Paige earned his nickname "Satchel."

Link to this Internet site from http://www.myreportlinks.com

▶ **Today In History: When You Pray, Move Your Feet**
At this Library of Congress Web site, you will learn about the fifty-four-mile civil rights march from Selma to Montgomery in 1965. Protesters marched for the rights of African Americans to vote and to commemorate the death of Jimmie Lee Jackson, a black man killed by state troopers. *Link to this Internet site from http://www.myreportlinks.com*

▶ **The Torchbearer: Rosa Parks**
By refusing to give up her seat to a white man on a Montgomery city bus in 1955, Rosa Parks sparked the modern American civil rights movement. Here you will find a biography of Mrs. Parks.

Link to this Internet site from http://www.myreportlinks.com

▶ **University of Alabama Museums: Moundville Archaeological Park**
Eight hundred years ago, Moundville was North America's largest city. Moundville Archaeological Park is located on the site of this once-thriving agricultural center. The park's Web site contains archaeological and visitor information. *Link to this Internet site from http://www.myreportlinks.com*

▶ **Welcome to the Birmingham Museum of Art**
The Birmingham Museum of Art contains more than 21,000 works of art from 5000 B.C. to the present. At their Web site you can obtain visitor information and take a virtual tour of their galleries.

Link to this Internet site from http://www.myreportlinks.com

Any comments? Contact us: comments@myreportlinks.com

Alabama Facts

▶ **Gained Statehood**
December 14, 1819, the twenty-second state

▶ **Capital**
Montgomery

▶ **Bird**
Yellowhammer

▶ **Motto**
Audemus jura nostra defendere ("We Dare Defend Our Rights")

▶ **Flower**
Camellia

▶ **Gemstone**
Star blue quartz

▶ **Tree**
Southern longleaf pine

▶ **Nicknames**
Yellowhammer State, The Heart of Dixie

▶ **Amphibian**
Red Hills salamander

▶ **Population**
4,447,100*

▶ **Song**
"Alabama" (words by Julia S. Tutwiler; music by Edna Gockel Gussen)

▶ **Insect**
Monarch butterfly

▶ **Fossil**
Basilosaurus cetoides

▶ **Reptile**
Alabama red-bellied turtle

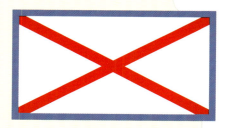

▶ **Flag**
Alabama's flag is a white field with a crimson St. Andrew's cross. The bars making up the cross cannot be less than six inches in width. They must extend from one side of the flag to the other.

*Population reflects the 2000 census.

10

Chapter 1 ▶

The State of Alabama

Alabama is a state of diverse land regions, impressive productivity, and historical significance. Because it sits in the center of the eleven southern states, Alabama is called the Heart of Dixie. American Indian influence is seen widely throughout Alabama in the many counties and rivers that have different American Indian names. For instance, the state of Alabama is named after the Alibamu

▲ Small churches like this old brick church in Mooresville, Alabama, can still be found throughout the state.

Indians, early farmers who cleared thickets in order to plant crops.

The Heart of Dixie

Alabama has a population of 4,447,100 people, ranking it the twenty-third most populated state. Most Alabamians live in cities where jobs in manufacturing and service industries are available. Montgomery is the state capital, and Birmingham is the state's largest city. Twenty-five percent of Alabama's residents are of African-American descent; yet Irish Americans, German Americans, and people descended from many other nationalities call Alabama home as well. Modern Alabamians, many the descendants of pioneers, are proud of their heritage and honor their ancestors by keeping pioneer traditions, crafts, and culture alive.

Geographically, Alabama is the thirtieth largest state. Six major land regions support agriculture, mining, or manufacturing. Alabama is the only state to have all the natural resources—coal, iron ore, and limestone—needed to make iron and steel. The marble produced in east-central Alabama is among the finest in the world. The state's 22 million acres of pine forest provide trees for logging and paper manufacturing. The rich fertile earth of the "Black Belt," southern Alabama's prairie land, supports the growth of crops and livestock. The fishing industry drives the economy in southern Alabama's Gulf of Mexico region.

A State of Historical Importance

Alabama became a territory in 1817 and, in 1819, became the twenty-second state to join the Union. Between 1860 and 1861, eleven southern states, including Alabama, seceded from the United States and formed the

Confederate States of America. Montgomery served as the first capital of the Confederacy, earning it the name "Cradle of the Confederacy." Nearly every white male Alabamian old enough to carry a rifle took part in the war.[1] The men in one Alabama regiment put yellow patches on the arms of their gray uniforms and were told they looked like yellowhammers, birds also known as common flickers. Because of this, Alabama was given yet another nickname, the Yellowhammer State.

Nearly one hundred years later, Montgomery was the site of yet another historical event. In 1955, Rosa Parks, an African-American woman, refused to give up her seat on a Montgomery bus to a white man. Her refusal fueled the civil rights movement. Montgomery became known as the Birthplace of the Civil Rights Movement.

The yellowhammer, or common flicker, is the state bird of Alabama. The name "yellowhammers" was given to Confederate soldiers from Alabama because they wore yellow patches on their sleeves.

▶ Something for Everyone

Alabama's recreational activities offer something for everyone. For nature lovers, Alabama has beaches along the Gulf Coast, miles of rivers, and many lakes for swimming, canoeing, and fishing. Each spring, the thirty-five-mile-long Azalea Trail blooms as it winds its way past historic homes and gardens of Mobile. With lakes, a gorge, and waterfalls, Oak Mountain State Park in Birmingham is one of Alabama's most beautiful areas. The park has horseback riding, golfing, and biking and hiking trails spread out over 9,940 acres. A demonstration farm where visitors can observe livestock being cared for and crops being grown and harvested is on site.

Alabama's national treasures offer a glimpse of the past. At Russell Cave, located near Bridgeport, the bones and cooking utensils of the cliff-dwelling Indians who lived in the Alabama region are displayed. Civil War buffs will find Alabama rich in landmarks that signify the role the state played before, during, and after the War Between the States (as the Civil War is often referred to in the South). Beautiful *antebellum* homes and plantations (*antebellum* referring to the years before the Civil War) can be found throughout the state. Fort Tyler, located in the city of Lanett on the Alabama-Georgia border, was the site of one of the last Civil War battles fought east of the Mississippi River. In Decatur, Morgan County, visitors can walk the National Trust Civil War Tour and take a self-guided tour of Civil War sites.

The Birmingham Civil Rights Institute focuses on more recent history. The museum, which is listed on the Register of Historic Sites, provides historical perspectives on America's civil rights movement. Huntsville, the state capital for one

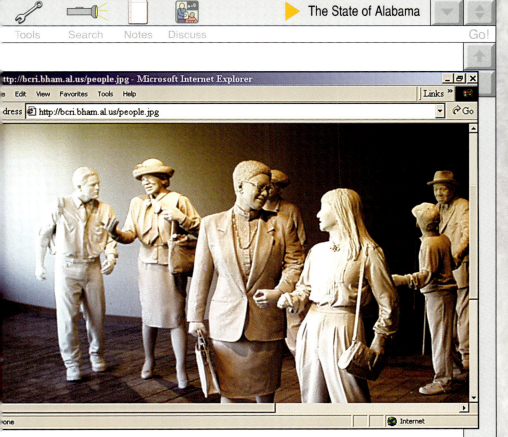

▲ These life-sized figures are posed to take a "walk of freedom" in the Processional Gallery of the Birmingham Civil Rights Institute.

year (1819), is called Rocket City USA because the United States Space and Rocket Center is located there. The *Saturn V*, the only rocket to put a human on the moon, was developed at the Marshall Space Flight Center. Space scientists at the center continue to study factors that affect future space exploration. Young people may attend the center's space camp to learn about space travel.

▶ A State of "Firsts"

Alabama is a state of "firsts." The country's first city-wide electrical streetcar system began operating in

Montgomery in 1886. Early in the 1900s, musician W. C. Handy, a native of Florence, introduced a new type of music, the soulful, melodic Blues. The tradition of Mardi Gras, the pre-Lenten celebration often identified with New Orleans, has its American origins in Mobile.

Many people who have inspired change and reform have lived in Alabama. Booker T. Washington, a former slave, saw a need for the education of African Americans after slavery was ended. In 1881, Washington founded Tuskegee Normal and Industrial Institute in Tuskegee. It is now known as Tuskegee University. One of the school's most renowned teachers was George Washington Carver, who became an internationally known agricultural

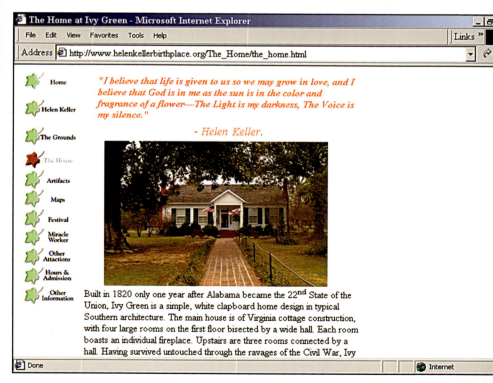

▲ One of the first great advocates for people with disabilities, Helen Keller was born in this home in Tuscumbia, Alabama.

chemist. Helen Keller, born in Tuscumbia, became blind, deaf, and mute from an illness when she was nineteen months old. Despite these obstacles, she learned to speak, went to college, wrote books, and became known the world over as an advocate for people with disabilities. Author Harper Lee, from Monroeville, wrote a book called *To Kill a Mockingbird*. It is the story of an African American wrongly accused of a crime in a small Alabama town, and of the white lawyer who defended him. The author won a Pulitzer Prize in 1961.

The Home of Legendary Athletes

Alabamians have made significant contributions to the sports world. In fact, three of the most famous members of the National Baseball Hall of Fame were born in Alabama. In 1974, Henry "Hank" Aaron, born in Mobile, broke Babe Ruth's home-run record. Willie Mays, from Westfield, was one of the greatest hitters and fielders of all time. And the legendary Leroy "Satchel" Paige, born in Mobile, was the first player from the Negro Leagues to be inducted into the Baseball Hall of Fame. Paige, known for his wit, threw more than fifty no-hitters during his long career, which included stints with three major league teams.

Alabama was also the home of another great athlete. Jesse Owens, from Danville, won four gold medals at the Berlin Olympics in 1936. Known as the world's fastest man, his accomplishments at Berlin in 1936 made him popular with everyone but Adolf Hitler, Germany's Nazi leader at the time. Hitler had attempted to use the games to prove his theories of "white superiority," but the impressive victories by Owens, a black man, interfered with those plans.

Chapter 2

Land and Climate

Alabama is a state of diverse geography. It borders on Georgia, Florida, Tennessee, and Mississippi. In its southwest corner is the Gulf of Mexico. The Appalachian Mountains, descending from Tennessee, cut across the state's northeast corner and extend almost to its center. Forests, lakes, plains, and rivers are terrains found in Alabama.

▶ Short Winters and Long, Hot Summers

Although the weather varies between the northern and southern parts of Alabama, in general, the state experiences a mild climate for much of the year. Northern Alabama experiences more seasonal changes than does the rest of the state. The leaves of trees in northern Alabama explode in a brilliance of color that peaks late in October. In this northern region, as in most of the state, the winter season lasts about two months—December and January. Winter temperatures in northern Alabama average about 46°F (8°C), and in southern Alabama, winter temperatures are generally above 50°F (10°C).

Snow falls on the highest elevations of the Appalachian Mountains in northeast Alabama. It is here that the coldest temperatures in the state are found. Around two to three inches of snow may fall during winters in areas north of Birmingham, although a "super storm" in March 1993 left much of northern Alabama buried under twenty-four inches of snow. Central and southern Alabama rarely see any snow.

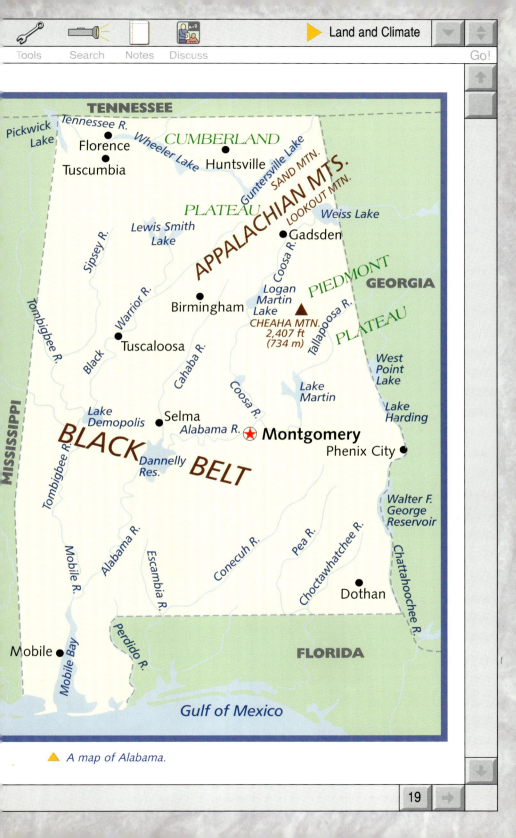

▲ A map of Alabama.

By March, spring is at its peak in Alabama, with daytime temperatures in the 70s throughout much of the state. Summers start in May and are long and hot. Summer temperatures throughout the state average about 80°F and often rise to 90°F and above. While there is no designated rainy season in Alabama, there are times during the winter and spring in northern Alabama when rain falls nearly every day. In southern Alabama, especially near the Gulf Coast, summer rainfall is abundant. The average rainfall for the state is fifty inches per year, with the Gulf Coast receiving approximately sixty-five inches per year.

The Gulf Coast is the warmest part of Alabama. There the climate is hot, humid, and wet, with gentle breezes along the coastline. June through November is hurricane season, and many storms, originating in the Atlantic Ocean and Caribbean Sea, gather force as they race along the Gulf Coast. Tornadoes occasionally touch down in the state, especially in central Alabama.

▶ The Gulf of Mexico

Mobile Bay, a picturesque harbor, is typical of the Gulf of Mexico coastline, which also

◀ At Fairhope, Alabama, this pier extends into the waters of the Gulf of Mexico.

consists of small bays and inlets. Dauphin Island is just one of the many islands that lie at the mouth of Mobile Bay. Perdido Bay sits on the Alabama-Florida border. Between the two bays lies the long, sandy peninsula of Alabama's Gulf Coast, which stretches for fifty-three miles (eighty-five kilometers). Including the inlets and small bays, Alabama has more than six hundred miles of tidal coastline.

Alabama's natural bottom offshore is flat and sandy. To protect the coastline, artificial reefs have been constructed from cement rubble and other recycled debris. Over time, the debris takes on the appearance of natural reefs, attracting red snapper and grouper fish. Alabama's artificial reef program is the largest in the United States.[1]

The sandy beaches, thick pine forests, and rolling grasslands of southern Alabama give way to tree-covered hills, ridges, and mountains in the north. Plant life has been abundant in the state for centuries. In 1843, Harvard botanist Asa Gray wrote of his trip down the southern Appalachians that trails led "through regions which abound with the choicest botanical treasures which the country affords."[2] Alabama has embarked on a program of wildflower preservation and beautified its roadways with thousands of brilliantly colored species. It is easy to see why the signs posted on the interstate highways leading into the state welcome visitors to "Alabama the Beautiful."

Diverse Land Regions

Alabama has a varied terrain. Its land slopes gradually from the mountains of the northeast to the coastal plain in the southwest. Most of the southern part of the state lies less than 500 feet above sea level. Alabama's lowest point is the

◀ The colors of fall in Alabama are captured in this scene of Borden Creek, in the Bankhead National Forest.

city of Mobile, which is at sea level. Cheaha Mountain, located on Piedmont's northwestern edge and the highest elevation in Alabama, rises to a height of 2,407 feet.

Alabama is divided into six land regions: the Cumberland Plateau, the Interior Low Plateau, the Piedmont, the Appalachian Ridge and Valley, the East Gulf Coastal Plain, and the Black Belt. The Cumberland Plateau, also known as the Appalachian Plateau, runs from Alabama's border with Georgia and Tennessee through the north-central part of the state. Known locally as the Cumberland Mountains, this area is also part of the Appalachian Mountains. The Appalachians originate in the Canadian province of Quebec and end in northern Alabama. Land elevations in the Cumberland Plateau vary greatly and range from eighteen hundred feet above sea level in its northeast section to five hundred feet in the southwest section.

The Interior Low Plateau in the northwest consists of fertile farmland fed by water from the Tennessee River. In the center of the state, extending to the east toward Georgia, is the forested area of the Piedmont. This area has many low hills and high ridges separated by sandy valleys. The Piedmont contains much of Alabama's natural resources of coal, iron ore, limestone, and marble.

These resources are also found in the Appalachian Ridge and Valley region, located north and slightly west of the Piedmont.

The East Gulf Coastal Plain is Alabama's largest land region, extending through most of the southern two thirds of the state. This land region is further divided into four sections. In the swamps and bayous of the Mobile River Delta, alligators make their homes. The Wiregrass Area in the southeast is named for the coarse grass that once grew in the pine forests. The northern part of the East Gulf Coastal Plain is called the Central Pine Belt because of its numerous pine forests. The Western Sandy Plain contains sandy soil, which is bad for growing crops.

The Black Belt is a narrow strip of rich farmland found in the center of the East Gulf Coastal Plain. It takes its name from the black fertile soil that supported the

The camellia is the state flower of Alabama.

growth of "King Cotton" on large plantations in the eighteenth and nineteenth centuries.

▶ Rivers, Lakes, and Dams

Twenty-six rivers provide Alabama with water for recreation, power, and industry. With more than sixteen hundred miles of rivers, Alabama ranks first among all fifty states in the number of miles of navigable river.[3] The state has two major river systems. Forty-four miles north of Mobile, Alabama's two longest rivers, the Alabama and the Tombigbee, come together to form the Mobile River. The Mobile River flows southward into the Gulf of Mexico. The Alabama River begins where the Coosa and Tallapoosa rivers flow together northeast of Montgomery. The Tombigbee River originates

▲ *The Horton Mill Bridge, one of eleven covered bridges remaining in Alabama, is also the highest covered bridge in the United States that spans a body of water. It is seventy feet above the Little Warrior River, in Blount County.*

in northeast Mississippi and flows southeast into Alabama. The Black Warrior River is the Tombigbee's main tributary. The Mobile and the Tensaw rivers flow into Mobile Bay, where they form two large deltas.

The southeastern section of Alabama is drained by a river system that is independent of the state's other river systems. The Pea, the Choctawhatchee, and the Conecuh rivers flow into Florida. The Chattahoochee River forms part of the border between Alabama and Georgia.

Several smaller rivers flow through the state. The Cahaba River is known as Alabama's "most floated" river because its natural beauty makes it a favorite waterway for tourists.

The Tennessee River enters Alabama's northeast corner from Tennessee. It flows across almost the entire width of northern Alabama in a westward loop before it reenters Tennessee. The Tennessee River has many dams that generate electrical power for the Cumberland Plateau. Dams along other rivers control flooding, and a system of locks keep rivers open to navigation. Wilson Dam, named for President Woodrow Wilson, began generating hydroelectric power from the Tennessee River in 1925. The Tennessee Valley Authority, a government agency formed during the Great Depression to provide work for the unemployed, operates the hydroelectric plants.

There are no large naturally occurring lakes in the state of Alabama. However, dams on many rivers throughout the state have formed a number of artificial lakes. The largest artificial lake in Alabama is Guntersville Lake, which covers 110 square miles. The Coosa River supports five lakes: Weiss, Lay, Mitchell, Jordan, and Logan Martin.

Chapter 3: Economy

The Civil War, the Industrial Revolution, and a boll weevil plague all played roles in defining Alabama's economy. At one time the crop was so important to the state's economy that Alabama was called the Cotton State.

Modern Alabama's gross state product, or the total value of all goods and services produced in one year, comes mainly from service industries. Manufacturing, agriculture, and mining also greatly contribute to Alabama's economy.

▶ A Changing Economy

There are many reasons why "King Cotton" ruled Alabama's economy prior to the Civil War. Alabama's mild climate, the fertile soil of its Black Belt, slave labor, and Eli Whitney's cotton gin combined to make cotton a profitable crop. The Civil War left many Alabamian cotton plantations in ruins. Those not destroyed were worked by former slaves for wages or were sharecropped—farmed in return for a share of the crops produced.

Sharecropping barely provided enough for families to survive. Late in the 1800s, industry began replacing some of Alabama's economic losses caused by the decline in cotton production. The Industrial Revolution was sweeping across the United States, and Alabama's rich store of minerals gave the state a head start in industrialization. Manufacturing now represents a large percentage of the state's economy.

▲ *The Battle-Friedman House in Tuscaloosa, now owned by the Tuscaloosa County Preservation Society, was built by a wealthy planter in 1835 who went on to lose most of his fortune following the Civil War.*

▶ A State of Services

Alabama's public school system is the state's largest employer. Education is considered a service industry. The service industries are a group of industries that help communities, businesses, and individuals. These jobs are located mainly in cities and suburbs. Retail and wholesale trade, health care, legal firms, communications, utilities, and computer services are examples of Alabama's service industries.

Birmingham, Alabama's financial center, is home to many banking, insurance, and real estate firms. Alabama has developed its own cyber-source for information, the Alabama Supercomputer Center. A supercomputer located in Cummings Research Park can be accessed by businesses, industries, and colleges.

Many Alabamians are employed in federal government offices in Montgomery and on military bases, such as Maxwell Air Force Base in Montgomery. The major employers in Huntsville are the George C. Marshall Space Flight Center and the Redstone Arsenal.

▶ Transportation

The transportation industry is another large employer of Alabamians. The state's shipping industry is based in Mobile, Alabama's only seaport and one of the busiest in the nation. Thirty-five oceangoing ships can be docked at Mobile at the same time.

Alabama has ninety public and eleven commercial airports. Ninety thousand miles of roadways, including five interstate highways, crisscross the state. Five thousand miles of railroad tracks connect Alabama's cities.

▶ Manufacturing and Mining

Coal, iron ore, and limestone, the three components needed to produce iron and steel, are found in the Appalachian Ridge and Valley region, near Birmingham. The iron and steel are used to produce transportation equipment, such as cars, trucks, airplane parts, and components for military and space equipment. Chemicals, fertilizers, and insecticides, Alabama's leading manufactured products, are produced in Decatur and Mobile. Alabama's lush forests provide the natural resources to manufacture the paper, cardboard, and paper bags that are produced in the mills of Mobile, Montgomery, and Childersburg. Food, textiles, plastics, electronics, and wood products are among the many other items manufactured in Alabama.

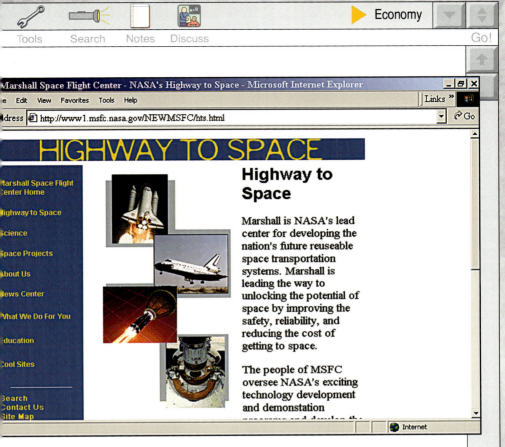

▲ The George C. Marshall Space Flight Center in Huntsville, part of NASA, was established in 1960. It is named for the army chief of staff during World War II whose efforts to rebuild war-torn Europe earned him the Nobel Peace Prize.

Most of Alabama's coal comes from the north-central part of the state. Alabama's coal is bituminous, or soft coal, and is found both underground and in surface mines. It is used to make methane gas in west-central Alabama.

Southwestern Alabama produces petroleum and natural gas. Alabama also mines limestone, bauxite, marble, clay, salt, sand, and gravel. The rising cost of petroleum and natural gas in the United States has placed an even greater importance on Alabama's coal.

▶ Land and Sea

Agriculture continues to make a valuable contribution to the productivity of the state. Most farms are located in the Cumberland Plateau, the Interior Low Plateau, and the Black Belt.

In 1915, a boll weevil plague spread across the southern part of the United States, and Alabama's cotton crop was ruined. The boll weevil is a beetle that feeds on the blossom, also called the boll, of the cotton plant. By necessity, farmers turned to other crops to make a living. Looking back, many Alabamians see the boll weevil plague as a blessing. The plague forced farmers to become more productive by using their land to grow new crops. In 1919, people in the city of Enterprise erected a monument to the pest.

Cotton is once again Alabama's main crop, but peanuts, corn, soybeans, wheat, potatoes, tomatoes, sweet potatoes, and watermelons are also grown on Alabama's forty-five thousand farms.

Three quarters of Alabama's farm income comes from livestock production. Broilers (young chickens between five and twelve weeks old) are the state's most important agricultural product. Beef cattle and hogs as well as eggs and milk contribute to Alabama's farm income. Grain-fed catfish are raised on farms in artificial ponds.

The fishing industry is also important to Alabama's economy. The state's annual catch is worth approximately $50 million. It comes mostly from the Gulf of Mexico. The shrimp harvest makes up the largest share of the salt-water economy, followed by blue crabs and oysters. Freshwater catches from rivers and lakes include buffalo fish, catfish, and mussels.

▲ When a boll weevil infestation struck Alabama's cotton fields, it forced the state's farmers to turn to other crops and to invest more in manufacturing, which benefited the state's economy. The town of Enterprise even erected a monument to the insect pest.

▶ Higher Education

Alabama offers a variety of opportunities for post high-school education. Students from all over the United States and many foreign countries attend colleges and universities in Alabama. The state has many private colleges, such as Tuskegee University in Tuskegee and Talladega College near Montgomery. Many of Alabama's private colleges are Christian colleges, such as Judson College in Marian, Faulkner University in Montgomery, and the University of Mobile in Mobile. Alabama's sixteen four-year public colleges offer the latest educational opportunities, including distance learning via computer. Auburn University, Alabama's largest university, has an enrollment of twenty-two thousand students. Athens State University, in Athens, is Alabama's oldest university. The University of Alabama is located in Tuscaloosa. A system of two-year state colleges, two veterinary schools, four law schools, and two medical schools are also part of Alabama's higher education offerings.

Tourism and Recreational Activities

Tourism is also a vital part of Alabama's economy. Annual events such as Mardi Gras in Mobile, the Dixie Cup Regatta in Guntersville, and Alabama Deep-Sea Fishing Rodeo at Dauphin Island draw thousands of tourists. The beaches along the Gulf of Mexico and the artificial lakes provide tranquil sites for recreational activities. Alabama's mild climate and varied terrain provide many opportunities for camping, hunting, fishing, canoeing, hiking, and biking. Twenty-four Alabama state parks offer facilities for boating, tennis, and golf, among other activities. Many of the state parks have caves where those who enjoy spelunking —the exploration of caves—can indulge in this pastime.

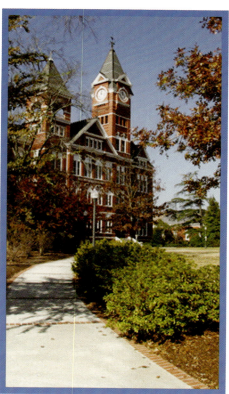

Samford Hall, on the campus of Auburn University.

There is much in Alabama that commemorates history. Tourists can learn firsthand about the struggle for civil rights by visiting the Rosa Parks Museum in Montgomery, the Civil Rights Institute in Birmingham, and the National Voting Rights Museum in Selma. History lovers can also visit Confederate Memorial Park in Marbury, the first White House of the Confederacy in Montgomery, and preserved antebellum estates and cotton plantations throughout Alabama.

Alabama's sporting events also contribute to the economy. Each year, the Crimson Tide, the University of Alabama's football team, plays the Auburn Tigers, the Auburn University team, in the Iron Bowl. Alabama has three minor-league baseball teams: the Huntsville Stars, the Birmingham Barons, and the Mobile BayBears. Many baseball games are played at the Hank Aaron Field, named after the Baseball Hall of Fame legend.

NASCAR fans from around the world come to Alabama to watch races on the Talladega Superspeedway, located near Birmingham. The Robert Trent Jones Golf Trail offers 378 holes of public golfing at nine sites stretched over 100 miles. The Alabama Sports Hall of Fame in Birmingham honors all the sports legends from the state.

Tourists and residents enjoy Alabama's music and fine arts. Birmingham and Huntsville have symphony orchestras, and Mobile has an opera company. The state has several theater and dance groups. The Birmingham Museum of Art is one of the premier regional art museums in the United States. It displays items spanning the years from 5,000 B.C. to the present. The Alabama Shakespeare Festival, located in Montgomery, is the sixth-largest Shakespeare festival in the world.[1]

Chapter 4

Government

Alabama, like many of its southern state neighbors, favored Democratic politicians on the national, state, and local levels until the mid-1900s, when a number of Republicans were elected to local positions as well as to the United States Congress. In the presidential election of 1964, most Alabamians voted for the Republican candidate, Barry M. Goldwater. It was the first time since 1872 that Alabamians supported a Republican presidential candidate. In 1986, Guy Hunt became the first Republican since the 1870s to be elected governor of Alabama.

▶ A Lengthy Constitution

Alabama has had six state constitutions. The present constitution was adopted in 1901. Whenever the voters of Alabama wish to change an aspect of government, they must amend their constitution. There are two ways to amend the constitution in Alabama. The Alabama state legislature can propose an amendment, but a three-fifths majority must approve it. Then Alabamians vote on the issue. An amendment may also be proposed by calling a constitutional convention. A majority of the members sitting in both houses of the Alabama legislature and a majority of the voters must approve the calling of a constitutional convention. The amendment proposed by the convention must then be approved by a majority of voters in an election.

Alabama's constitution has been amended over seven hundred times. More amendments have been added to the constitution of Alabama than to that of any other state. A group of Alabamians is looking at ways to make it easier for changes to be made to the state constitution. Their work is called the Constitution Project.

▶ The Branches of State Government

Alabama's government is divided into three branches. The executive branch consists of a governor who serves a four-year term. The governor can serve more than one term, but not three terms in a row. The governor must be at least thirty years old. Alabama's executive branch also includes a lieutenant governor, secretary of state, attorney general, auditor, treasurer, and commissioner of agriculture and industries. All of these government officials serve terms of four years.

The state legislative branch includes a 35-member senate and a 105-member house of representatives. State representatives serve four-year terms. Nationally, two senators and seven members of the House of Representatives represent Alabama. The state exercises nine electoral votes in presidential elections.

The judicial branch of the government encompasses a state supreme court, the highest court in Alabama, and lower courts. A chief justice and eight associate judges sit on Alabama's supreme court. Their term of office is six years. There is also a court of civil appeals and a court of criminal justice. Alabama's lower courts consist of circuit courts, district courts, parole courts, and municipal courts.

▶ Local Government in Alabama

On the local level, the state is made up of sixty-seven counties. A board of commissioners, also known as county commissions, oversees each county. County government

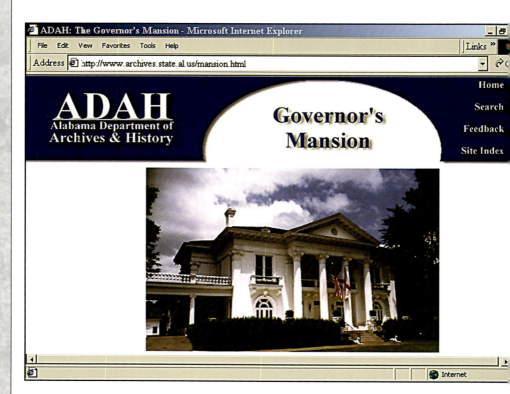

▲ An official residence for the governor of Alabama did not exist until 1911. The present residence of the state's chief executive, pictured above, was purchased in 1950 from the estate of General Robert Fulwood Ligon.

consists of a probate judge, sheriff, superintendent of education, district attorney, engineer, and tax collector. The probate judge serves a term of six years. A mayor and city council govern larger cities such as Birmingham, Montgomery, and Huntsville. A few of Alabama's smaller cities are governed by a city manager.

▶ State Government Funding

Approximately 50 percent of the Alabama state government's income is generated from federal funding and the interest earned on public accounts. The other 50 percent comes from taxes. Alabama supports many of its state programs with the revenue collected from personal and corporate income taxes and sales and use taxes. Alabama also taxes alcoholic beverages, insurance premiums, public utilities, motor vehicle licenses, business licenses, and public utilities.

A Roaming Capital

Since becoming a territory of the United States in 1817, Alabama has had five capital cities.[1] St. Stephens served as the territorial capital. Huntsville was the capital for Alabama's first constitutional convention. Cahaba was Alabama's capital from 1820 to 1825. Tuscaloosa was the capital from 1826 to 1846. Montgomery, which is located more centrally, replaced Tuscaloosa as the capital in 1847. Two years later, Montgomery's newly constructed capitol building was destroyed by a fire. The central section of the present capitol building was built on the foundation of the destroyed building.

Alabamians are interested in government on all levels and actively participate in studying and endorsing issues that improve the quality of life in their state.

Chapter 5 ▶

History

Scientists believe humans have lived on the land that is now Alabama since 8000 B.C. These early people were nomads who lived in caves and on cliffs. They hunted large animals for food with sharpened bones and rocks, and they also ate berries. Eventually, they formed tribes. Sometime between A.D. 800 and 1500, the tribes settled down in villages. At the center of each village were sixty-foot-high mounds. The villagers have been named mound builders and belong to what archaeologists call the Mississippi Culture. Often, the home of the tribe's leader was built on top of a mound, which also served as the village's sacred burial place. Mound builders disappeared by the beginning of the seventeenth century, although archaeologists do not understand why. Artifacts from their culture, such as tools, jewelry, and weapons, are on exhibit at the Jones Archeological Museum in Moundville Archaeological Park, near Tuscaloosa. The descendants of the mound builder society were the Creek, Chickasaw, and Choctaw tribes. These tribes spoke Muskogean. The Iroquois-speaking Cherokee tribe later joined them.

▶ The Spanish and French Explorers

The Spanish were the first explorers to reach Alabama. Alonso Alvarez de Pineda sailed into Mobile Bay in 1519. Hernando de Soto landed in Florida in 1539 and marched through several southern states in pursuit of gold, reaching Alabama in 1540. In Alabama, bloody battles raged between de Soto and the American Indians under Chief

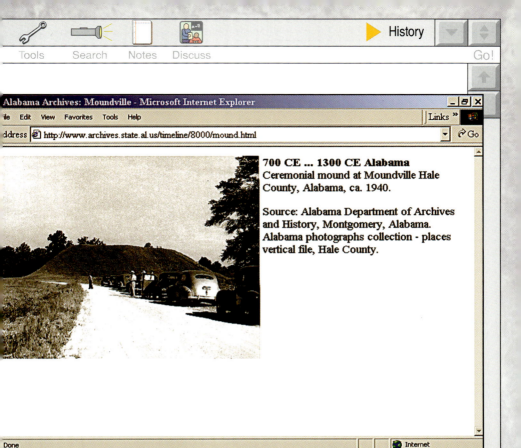

▲ This photograph from the 1940s shows a ceremonial mound in Hale County, probably built between A.D. 700 and 1300. It is believed that the homes of ancient tribal leaders were built upon such mounds.

Tuscaloosa, whose name means "Black Warrior." Although de Soto was victorious over the natives, he and his explorers did not settle in Alabama. Another Spanish explorer, Tristan de Luna, attempted to start a colony near Mobile Bay in 1559, but abandoned the area. In 1682, René-Robert Cavelier, Sieur de La Salle, traveled down the Mississippi River from Canada to the Gulf of Mexico. La Salle named the land he claimed for France, including Alabama, the Louisiana Territory, after France's king Louis XIV. The king sent two brothers, Pierre Le Moyne, Sieur d'Iberville, and Jean-Baptiste Le Moyne, Sieur de

Bienville, to establish a colony of French settlers in Alabama. In 1702, they founded Alabama's French territorial capital at Fort Louis de la Mobile. In 1711, a flood destroyed Fort Louis, and the capital was moved to present-day Mobile. The French settlers established plantations to grow sugar and rice. The plantations flourished with the labor of enslaved Africans, who were first brought to Alabama early in the 1700s.

The increasing numbers of British settlers in lands held by the French led to the French and Indian War (1754–63). The Treaty of Paris, in 1763, forced France to surrender Mobile to the British. After the Revolutionary War (1775–83), northern Alabama became part of the United States, while southern Alabama remained under Spanish rule. Spain ceded part of Alabama to the French in 1800, but kept Mobile. France sold this land as part of the Louisiana Purchase to the United States in 1803.

▶ Horseshoe Bend

As more white settlers came to Alabama early in the 1800s, there were frequent disputes with American Indians over territorial rights. Pioneers often settled on land previously inhabited by many tribes, particularly the Creek. During the War of 1812, Andrew Jackson, a general in the United States Army, fought the Creek over Alabamian land. One of his most significant battles was the Battle of Horseshoe Bend, fought on March 27, 1814. Nearly one thousand Creek warriors fought Jackson's force of more than three thousand American soldiers and Cherokee and Lower Creek tribes.[1] Jackson's victory forced the Creek to sign treaties calling for them to give up their land to the United States government.

The War of 1812 (1812–15) united Mobile with the rest of Alabama, and in 1819, Alabama became the twenty-second state in the union.

▶ The Civil War and Reconstruction

Alabama's economy was dependent upon cotton, which in turn was dependent upon slavery. Slavery was only one of several causes that resulted in Alabama's seceding and joining the Confederate States of America, in 1861. Montgomery was chosen as the first Confederate capital. During the Civil War (1861–65), Mobile Bay was the site

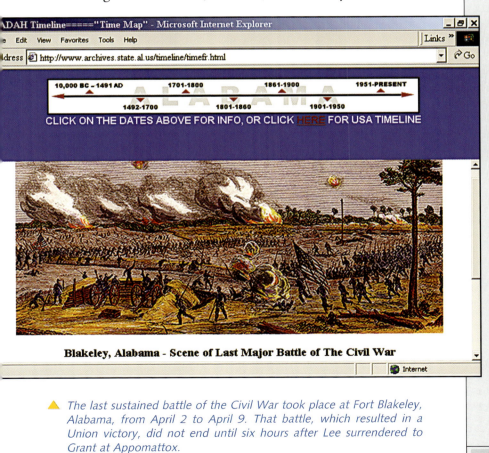

▲ The last sustained battle of the Civil War took place at Fort Blakeley, Alabama, from April 2 to April 9. That battle, which resulted in a Union victory, did not end until six hours after Lee surrendered to Grant at Appomattox.

of a decisive sea battle. In the Battle of Mobile Bay, on August 5, 1864, Admiral Farragut's Union ships successfully blocked food and supplies desperately needed by the Confederates.

During Reconstruction, the period that followed the Civil War, leaders of both the North and the South had to work toward becoming one nation again. The war left Alabama in political, social, and economic chaos. Laws called the Black Codes curtailed the freedoms of the newly freed slaves. During the years of Reconstruction, Alabama was governed by carpetbaggers (Northerners who had moved South after the war) and scalawags (Southerners who had opposed secession).

By the time the Federal government ended Reconstruction in 1877, Alabama had fallen under the rule of wealthy landowners who had favored secession, and the rights of former slaves were once again restricted.

▶ Two World Wars and a Depression

Alabama made a major contribution to the war effort during the years that the United States was involved in World War I (1917–18). Food and cotton grown in the state supplied civilians and military alike. Alabamian textile mills provided soldiers and sailors with uniforms, and steel mills produced ammunition and other items needed for war.

Ten years after World War I ended, Alabama, along with the rest of the nation, was affected by the Great Depression, which followed the stock market crash of 1929. The price of cotton decreased drastically. Many people lost their farms, and others became unemployed when Alabama's factories closed. Alabamians had to rely on help from the federal government for programs that

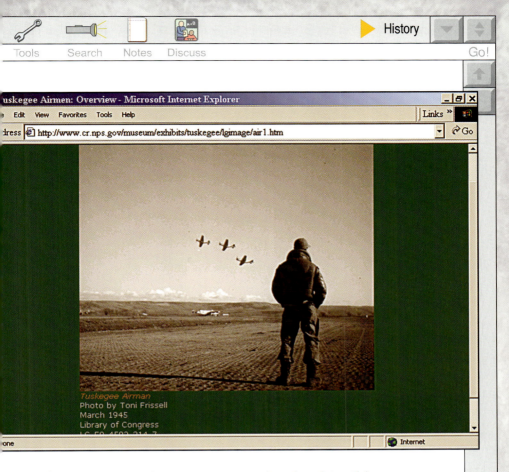

▲ In 1941, an African-American squadron based in Alabama was formed as the first such group allowed to fly military missions for the United States. Known as the Tuskegee Airmen because they trained at the Tuskegee Institute, the pilots, navigators, and others involved overcame prejudice to become one of the most respected squadrons of World War II.

brought work back into the state. The Tennessee Valley Authority was created to build dams along the Tennessee River. The dams also provided Alabamians with hydroelectric power.

With America's entrance into World War II in 1941, Alabama once again contributed to the war effort. It was in Alabama that the Army Air Corps (now known as the United States Air Force) set up an air force base at Tuskegee Army Air Field to train African-American pilots.

Those pilots became known as the Tuskegee Airmen. The outstanding military achievement of this corps of African-American pilots led to the integration of African Americans into all branches of the armed services.

▶ The Civil Rights Movement

Although African Americans were legally allowed to vote, their rights improved very little in the first half of the twentieth century. In 1901, the Alabama legislature enacted a law requiring each person who wished to vote to pay a poll tax. Anyone who could not afford to pay the tax was not allowed to vote. Segregation, the policy of separating African Americans from the rest of the population, was enforced in Alabama. When riding public transportation, African Americans were required to give up their seats to white people. Rosa Parks, an African-American woman, was arrested for refusing to give her bus seat to a white man on a Montgomery city bus in December 1955. That event led Dr. Martin Luther King, Jr., a Baptist preacher in Montgomery, to call for a boycott of the Montgomery public bus system. African Americans accounted for more than half of the city's bus ridership. The entire world watched as the nonviolent protest, led by Dr. King, unfolded in Montgomery. Dr. King later led civil rights marches from many of Alabama's key cities to the capital at Montgomery. King's protests in Birmingham in 1963, in which he was jailed, brought him to the world's attention. Alabama was thus center stage in the fight for civil rights, and its capital earned the title of the "Birthplace of the Civil Rights Movement."

After the United States Supreme Court outlawed segregation in the public schools in 1954, many Alabamians refused to acknowledge the rights of African Americans. In 1963, Alabama's governor George Wallace personally attempted to prevent African-American students from entering the University of Alabama. Federal marshals were called in and forced Governor Wallace to comply with integrating the schools.

By the end of the twentieth century, African Americans were taking on important roles of leadership in state and national affairs. In 2000, Alabama counted among its African American leadership one representative in Congress, eight state senators, and forty mayors.[2]

▶ Alabama Today

Alabama has undergone many social, political, and economic changes over the years, yet it remains a vibrant and strong state. Alabamians are a resilient people who honor their past while forging ahead into the future. A strong historical foundation for overcoming obstacles makes modern Alabamians ready to face the challenges of the twenty-first century. You could say the state has a lot of heart—the Heart of Dixie.

▶ This photograph of Rosa Parks was taken approximately ten years after she was arrested for refusing to give up her seat to a white passenger on a Montgomery city bus. Her courage and resolve sparked the Montgomery Bus Boycott.

Chapter Notes

Chapter 1. The State of Alabama

1. Harry Hansen, ed., *Alabama: A Guide to the Deep South* (New York: Hastings House Publishers, Inc., 1975), p. 42.

Chapter 2. Land and Climate

1. *Alabama Department of Conservation and Natural Resources, Marine Resources Division,* "Alabama's Artificial Reef Program—A Brief History," September 5, 2002, <http://www.dcnr.state.al.us/MR/reef_hist.htm>.

2. Charlton Ogburn, *The Southern Appalachians: A Wilderness Quest* (New York: William Morrow and Co., Inc., 1975), p. 156.

3. *Alabama Department of Archives and History,* "Alabama Moments in American History: Transportation and Alabama Rivers," September 9, 2002, <http:www.alabamamoments.state.al.us/sec06det.html>.

Chapter 3. Economy

1. *The Alabama Shakespeare Festival,* "About the Festival," n.d., <http://www.asf.net/history.html> (April 2, 2003).

Chapter 4. Government

1. *Alabama Department of Archives and History,* "Capitals of Alabama," n.d., <http://www.archives.state.al.us/capital/capitals.html> (April 2, 2003).

Chapter 5. History

1. *The National Park Service,* "The Battle of Horseshoe Bend—Determining the Facts: The Battle of Horseshoe Bend and Its Consequences," n.d., <http://www.cr.nps.gov/nr/twhp/wwwlps/lessons/54horseshoe/54facts3.htm> (September 9, 2002).

2. David A. Bositis, "Black Elected Officials: A Statistical Summary 2000," *Joint Center for Political and Economic Studies, 2002,* <http://www.jointcenter.org> (March 15, 2003).

Further Reading

Davis, Lucile. *Alabama.* Danbury, Conn.: Children's Press, 1999.

Feeney, Kathy. *Alabama.* Danbury, Conn.: Children's Press, 2002.

Greenfield, Eloise. *Rosa Parks.* New York: HarperCollins Children's Books, 1996.

Kavanagh, James. *Alabama Birds.* Chandler, Ariz.: Waterford Press, 1999.

Reger, James P. *Life in the South During the Civil War.* San Diego: Lucent Books, 1997.

Stein, R. Conrad. *The Montgomery Bus Boycott.* Chicago: Children's Press, 1993.

Thompson, Kathleen. *Alabama.* Austin, Tex.: Raintree Steck-Vaughn, 1991.

Wills, Charles A. *A Historical Album of Alabama.* Brookfield, Conn.: Millbrook Press, 1995.

Ziff, Marsha. *Reconstruction Following the Civil War.* Berkeley Heights, NJ: Enslow Publishers, Inc., 1999.

Index

A
Aaron, Henry, 17
Athens, Alabama, 32

B
Battle of Horseshoe Bend, 40
Battle of Mobile Bay, 42
Birmingham, 12, 14, 18, 27, 33, 36, 41
Bridgeport, 14, 28

C
Cahaba, 37
Carver, George Washington, 16–17
Cavelier, René-Robert, Sieur de La Salle, 39
Childersburg, 28
civil rights movement, 13, 14–15, 44–45
Civil War, 13, 14, 26, 41–42
climate, 18, 20
Creek wars, 40

D
Danville, 17
Dauphin Island, 21, 32
Decatur, 14, 28
De Luna, Tristan, 39
De Pineda, Alonso Alvarez, 38
De Soto, Hernando, 38–39

E
economy, 12, 26–33

F
Fort Louis de la Mobile, 40
Fort Tyler, 14
French and Indian War, 40

G
geographic regions
    Appalachian Ridge and Valley, 22–23, 28
    Black Belt, 22, 23–24, 26, 30
    Cumberland Plateau, 22, 30
    East Gulf Coastal Plain, 20, 22–23
    Interior Low Plateau, 22, 30
    Piedmont, 22–23
George C. Marshall Space Flight Center, 15, 28
government, 34–37

H
Handy, W. C., 16
higher education, 31–32
highest point (Cheaha Mountain), 22
history, 12–14, 26, 38–45

J
Jackson, Andrew, 40–41

K
Keller, Helen, 17
King, Dr. Martin Luther, Jr., 44

L
Le Moyne, Jean-Baptiste, 39–40
Le Moyne, Pierre, 39–40
Lee, Harper, 17
Louisiana Purchase, 40

M
Mays, Willie, 17
Mobile, 14, 16, 17, 22, 28, 31, 32, 33, 36, 41
Montgomery (state capital), 12, 16, 28, 36, 37, 42, 44

O
Owens, Jesse, 17

P
Paige, Leroy "Satchel," 17
Parks, Rosa, 13, 44

R
Revolutionary War, 40

S
Selma, 33

T
Tennessee Valley Authority, 25, 43
Tuscaloosa, Chief, 38–39
Tuscaloosa (city), 37, 38
Tuscumbia, 17
Tuskegee Institute, 16–17, 43–44

W
Wallace, George, 44–45
War of 1812, 41
Washington, Booker T., 16
waterways, 24–25
Wilson, Woodrow, 25
World War I, 42
World War II, 42–43